Battle Scars

Life After Breast Cancer

DeAnn Clark

ISBN (print): 978-0-9968290-3-8
ISBN (kindle): 978-0-9968290-4-5
ISBN (ebook): 978-0-9968290-5-2

Library of Congress Control Number: 2017901256

Author Photo: www.mindykerrphotography.com

Unless otherwise noted, scripture quotations are taken from the *Holy Bible, New Living Translation*. Copyright 1996, 2004. Used by permission of Tyndale House Publishers, Inc., Wheaton, Illinois 60189. All rights reserved.

To Contact the Author:

DeAnn Clark Ministries
P.O. Box 1623 | Palmetto, FL 34220
w w w . d e a n n c l a r k m i n i s t r i e s . c o m

Disclaimer

The author is not engaged in rendering professional advice or services to the individual reader. The ideas and suggestions in this book are not intended to be a substitute of any kind for consulting with your physician. Medical supervision is required in regard to all matters regarding your health. The author shall not be liable or responsible for any loss or damage allegedly arising from any information or suggestion in this book.

This book contains the opinions, ideas, and personal decisions of the author. It is solely for informational and educational purposes and should not be regarded as a substitute for professional medical treatment. Everyone's body and health situation is unique. Therefore, you should consult a health professional to guide you in making any decisions concerning your medical treatment options and to answer any questions about your situation.

Acknowledgements

I want to thank God for the work of the cross. The blood of Jesus not only paid for my sins, but by His stripes we are healed. I also want to thank my family, friends, my doctors and their medical teams for walking out every step of my journey with me. What the enemy meant for destruction God has turned into resounding victory.

Praise for Battle Scars

Battle Scars is a powerful encouragement to anyone who has or had breast cancer. The book is also a very powerful tool for family and friends of a breast cancer patient to assist them in how to cope and help the one they love walk through cancer. DeAnn gets raw and real with her experience about walking this sickness out and facing a demonic giant named cancer straight in the face, with the guidance of her Lord and Savior Jesus.

KARI STEPHENS PERKINS
Founder of Get Up & Get Real Ministry
www.getupandgetreal.org

Powerful, sobering, and at the same time encouraging for all who read this book. ***Battle Scars*** is a brave and compelling account of a journey through cancer and out to the other side. We can glean so much from DeAnn's experience in this personal, spiritual and very practical book.

ROBERT & HELEN KING
Pastors of Freedom Church in Wales UK
www.freedomchurchcwmbran.com

DeAnn Clark has done it again. Her raw passion and honesty has set forth a platform for people to truly deal with the difficult situations they face. ***Battle Scars*** provides a space for those who have faced, will face or know someone who has faced the "C" word to learn how to deal with it. What a hope DeAnn describes! As a minister, this will be a resource I keep on hand.

JACOB BISWELL
Founder of Jacob Biswell Ministries
Prophet, Author, Speaker
www.jacobbiswell.com

Battle Scars serves as testimony to how DeAnn was able to navigate her way emotionally from diagnosis of breast cancer to reconstruction and full recovery with faith as her anchor. As a therapist and as a survivor, I know that each of us has to discover our own path to victory. I have ready many books on the subject of breast cancer, but *Battle Scars* is the first I have encountered to address the shame a Christian can feel because they are battling this disease. DeAnn encourages us to have hope as we start our journey.

RITA EVANS, LCSW
Life Resources

You gain strength, courage, and confidence by every experience in which you really stop to look fear in the face.

—Eleanor Roosevelt

Contents

Cancer is a word, not a sentence.

—John Diamon

Foreword

He who overcomes, I will make him a pillar in the temple of My God, and he will not go out from it anymore; and I will write on him the name of My God, and the name of the city of My God, the new Jerusalem, which comes down out of heaven from My God, and My new name.

REVELATION 3:12 NASB

If there is never a battle, there is never a victory. There are going to be times when we walk through difficult seasons of sickness and pain. It is in this dark valley we must anchor our trust and confidence in Jesus alone. Jesus will never leave us or forsake us, and He will impart His strength to us as we face our adversities. He is the ultimate overcomer of hell and death and it is through Him alone that we also become overcomers.

This book is not only a testimony of DeAnn Clark and her personal struggle with breast cancer, but how she won the battle as an overcomer. How do we press our way past the enemy of fear to a place of rest, faith, and trust? How do we respond to a shocking diagnosis of a killer disease that only God can heal? I know, because I've been there too.

In 2007 Prophet John Paul Jackson invited my husband David and me to pastor and launch a church in his network. It was one of the highlights of our life and much to our delight we responded positively. Only a few days later we are suddenly faced with a shocking, life threatening diagnosis. My thought was, how can this be happening now? Why is this happening to me? Fear gripped my heart.

Because the Sovereign LORD helps me, I will not be disgraced. Therefore have I set my face like flint, and I know I will not be put to shame.

ISAIAH 50:7 NIV

I knew God was good. I knew Him as my healer and knew He loved all He has made. I knew He would not allow me to go through anything I could not endure.[1]

Fear, doubt, and unbelief makes everything worse. It tried to smother me until I launched an attack against it and pressed through. Now fear cannot move me anymore. I hold the keys of the overcomer! God knew ahead of time what my life would hold. He had already placed a way of escape there for me.

We all desire to be healed instantly by divine encounter, yet this is not always the case. It does happen (and if you are fighting right now, I pray that you are healed instantly), but God is with us no matter which way it happens. Instant healing or through a surgeon's hand ... both are miracles to me.

Today, ten years later I stand and testify that God healed me and I am cancer free for the glory of His name! He walked me through the valley of the shadow of death and I fear no evil, for He is with me.[2]

I praise Him daily for giving me the power to overcome in the battle and come through to the other side as a victorious warrior. He allowed me to go through the battle and win which gave Him just cause to promote me as an overcomer! I meet many women who have fought or are fighting the same battle, but now I have the authority to speak to them with power.

Even if healing alludes us this side of heaven, we all still win the battle. The moment we are with Jesus, our bodies are at last perfected, beautifully healed, and totally whole. On this earth, when we come through we have battle scars—proof that we have fought the good fight and lived to tell about it. On the other side of the battle we value life differently and reevaluate the importance of things. After staring death in the face, we are stronger and our trust is deeper.

If you are fighting a battle with cancer right now, be reassured: **God is fighting for you!** You will have the testimony of a mighty warrior. It's during the fight that God strengthens you on the inside in a way that could never happen otherwise. You must fight and not quit. The enemy does not lay down his weapon and declare a cease fire, he will simply run you over to eliminate you from victory. So fight you must.

Welcome to the battlefield. Let's run with courage and fight by never giving up. Let this book help you to be the overcomer you were meant to be. Live victoriously, fight for the crown, and receive your reward.

PASTOR RONDA RAMER, M.DIV.
Co-founder of Glory Fire International Ministries
Co-pastor of Glory Fire Church
www.gloryfirechurch.com

Endnotes

1. 1 Corinthians 10:13.
2. Psalm 23 (paraphrased).

Chapter One

The Day That Changed the World

I remember it like it was yesterday. I was sitting in a room across from someone I knew well and trusted much. My medical chart and new pathology report were in her hands. Her head was down as she held them, studying the contents of the report.

No big deal, I thought as I sat quietly waiting for her to give me the result I was expecting—totally benign; *no worries.* I was still sitting there rehearsing in my mind what she was going to say. When she opened her mouth I was ready for the good news!

Instead, the words she spoke crashed over me in crushing waves. I felt the room spin as the nightmarish twist in her findings stung and tore at my heart. In a moment of total shock and surprise, my thoughts went from joyful expectation to utter disbelief and chaos. It was as if all the air in the room—in the universe—disappeared, leaving me in a silent vacuum. I couldn't breathe. I couldn't think.

This can't be happening!

I looked around the room at all the beautiful décor. It all seemed foreign and strange to me. I fixed my eyes on the familiar things I brought with me, grasping for something, anything, safe and comforting that said **Nothing would ever be the same again.** this is not real. But nothing was the same as when I walked in. Nothing would ever be the same again. In the space of a moment, everything changed.

My mind spun in disbelief and dread. I was totally unprepared for this. *This can't be happening to me,* I thought. There must be some mistake.

I wanted her to stop talking. I wanted to make all this craziness go away. I could barely sit there, let alone listen. I could scarcely breathe.

If there had been any thought in my mind that I might receive a negative report, I would have at least asked someone to come with me. There I sat alone, listening to this trusted friend and doctor saying strange and horrifying things to me.

Our eyes met. I will never forget the sadness looking back at me as she said the words no one ever wants to hear, "DeAnn, you have cancer."

I had cancer. I am a breast cancer survivor.

I have a story to share. I understand what cancer does to you when it comes—not from a medical perspective, but from a woman's perspective.

I share my experience with you to bring you encouragement. I am saying to you, "You are not alone!" So, get yourself a cup of tea (or whatever your favorite beverage is), and let's talk.

Cancer is a word, not a sentence.

—John Diamon

Chapter Two

My Journey

If you or someone you love is actually walking out a similar diagnosis, I am telling you there is hope. There is love, and there is a very special practical kind of help through God Himself. God is never the one who puts cancer (or any other sickness) on you. You must get that settled in your mind and in your heart once and for all. In Heaven, there is no cancer or any disease at all.

The Bible tells us the devil comes to steal, kill, and destroy (John 10:10). Cancer is one of his tools, and I am here to "out him," to expose him, uncover him, and shout out, "Cancer is his dirty work!" This is serious stuff, and we need to know who we are in Christ when we are fighting it. We have weapons!

The discovery of a lump came in the first place for me because I wasn't feeling right. I wasn't feeling sick really, but everything tired me out. I asked God if there was something in my body that I needed to see. One night I was dressed for bed, and as I settled in for the night, I reached across myself to adjust my nightgown. That's when I first felt the lump! I reached again and felt it again. Oh no! What is this? I tried to make all the wild thoughts go away.

That night I slept off and on. The next day I made an appointment and went in to see my doctor. In trying to examine me, the doctor couldn't feel the lump, so she asked me to show her where it was. I had to put myself into a very strange position for her or the medical team to feel it. The doctor finally said, "It's probably nothing, but you need to check it out."

I was getting ready to head to a conference in Atlanta in a couple of weeks where I was scheduled to meet other ministers. Since I had lived in the Atlanta area for some time, all my medical records were still located there. So I made the effort to get an appointment at the Women's Center while I was there. I had to inform them that I had found a lump in order to be placed on their schedule so quickly.

The day of my appointment arrived and I found myself in the Women's Center, again having to show them where the lump was. It was difficult for them to locate; it didn't even show up in the mammography. I showed the technician how to find the lump, and when she did, her reaction startled me. She jerked her head up, took additional shots of that location, and took off down the hall to find the doctor. As I waited there, I thought, *Hmm ... that's not good.*

Immediately they moved me to the ultrasound lab. When I got there, the lady began talking to me and asked where the lump was. I showed her, too. As she moved the wand of the ultrasound and pressed down where I showed her, she had a startled reaction, snapped some magnified images, and immediately ran out of the room. (May I say here that this is disconcerting to go through by yourself.) I truly had no worries and was ready to hear the words this is no big deal. Before long the nurses returned with forms for me to sign for a needle biopsy to be done as soon as possible. *This is really not good,* I thought to myself.

I sat there with the doctor waiting and signed all the forms. *I am under so much stress and anxiety,* I thought, *how do they expect me to fully understand exactly what I'm signing?* Then I quietly sat and waited for them to call me in to go have the biopsy done. But then suddenly, there was a change of plans. Instead of doing the biopsy immediately, it had to be postponed because of an emergency in the ultrasound lab. So I was rescheduled for the next day.

More waiting …

I decided since I was in Atlanta anyway and the biopsy was put off until morning, I would still attend the conference that night. The other ministers were expecting me to be there; no one knew what I was doing medically. The Women's Center was clear across the city from the conference location and my hotel room. With all this weighing on my mind, I left the medical complex and decided to drive back across the city immediately to beat the traffic. That evening I participated in the conference and assisted the other ministers during ministry time.

The next morning I got up, and once again, drove across Atlanta to report in for the needle biopsy. This time they did it. They made their incision and performed the biopsy. (Don't let anyone tell you it's a needle biopsy; that thing looked like a crochet hook!) They put the steri-strips on me, and gave me ice bags. I was told to change the ice bag every so many hours, and they would call to check on me. And that was that. I left with the knowledge that they would call me with the results in a few days.

It all felt so surreal, cold, and impersonal. I felt very much alone. (I can honestly tell you, in many ways my journey was a lonely one. God never left me, though, not even for a second.) I walked through it matter-of-factly, but in a kind of vacuum. My head was numb. It was like it was happening to someone else, but it was me.

So there I was—alone in Atlanta, scheduled to help minister at the conference. I was left with two ice bags and some extras, along with a mind-numbing wait to learn the results of the biopsy. I drove back across the city, and that evening, I went to the conference wearing an ice bag on one side. When the bag warmed, I placed it on the other side and replaced it with another cold one to keep a balanced appearance in my clothes—one bag on each side with a jacket over everything. (Ladies, jackets hide a multitude of things!) They had to be changed every two hours. I was totally unprepared for all that. So I stood and ministered to people with ice bags in my bra! LOL!

I stood and ministered to people with ice bags in my bra!

I mentioned that I was told they would contact me in a couple of days with the biopsy results. When I didn't hear anything by the end of the conference, I moved into a hotel closer to the hospital to continue waiting. Since I lived in Florida, I decided to stay and wait for the report. I contacted some friends and had dinner with them the following night. I said nothing about what was going on.

Several days of waiting later, the phone finally rang. The news sounded good: the biopsy was normal. There were no cancer cells, and there were not even any pre-cancerous cells present in any of the tissue samples they had taken.

"Let this heal," the doctor said, "then within six months have the lump removed because of its location, just to be on the safe side." I should have been relieved. I wasn't. Within me I was thinking, *Okay, there was no cancer in the places where tissue samples were taken; but what about where they didn't sample?*

Within my spirit I heard the Holy Spirit say, "Get it done quickly. Don't wait."

Chapter Three

Lumpectomy

I waited only 30 days to have the lump removed. The surgeon did the lumpectomy in her office operating room using just a local anesthetic on me. We are friends, so we talked through the whole procedure. When she had the lump removed, she said, "I want you to feel this." (I've assisted in many surgeries through the years, and because of that, my surgeon said this to me.) She put a surgical glove on my hand, and handed the lump to me.

I was shocked when I felt it. I was expecting it to be the size of a small English pea, but it was about the size of the end joint of my thumb. It was that wide, too.

What I had felt that first night turned out to be only the tip of the iceberg, so to speak. "Why didn't it show up in the mammogram?" I asked aloud, my doctor shaking her head with no answer. "After all, they did four of them at the time."

I went home and I waited again.

A week later I returned to my surgeon's office. The results from the biopsy were in. The pathology from the lump revealed it was cancer, sure enough.

Bam! There it was. Cancer.

The enemy had been hiding. What I had heard in my spirit when I was given the original diagnosis of cancer-free was spot on: "Go get it removed; don't wait!"

I have learned to always listen to what the Holy Spirit speaks to me. It is vitally important to know what your spirit (your gut, whatever you want to call it) is saying to you. In that you will find the truth. You must know how to listen so you hear what He is saying to you. Listen to that small inner voice.

The next words from my doctor were, "We can do a mastectomy this week."

"Wait ... what? I said. My mind went numb. *From a simple lumpectomy to a mastectomy without any warning ... how can that be?* I just looked at them in shock and heard myself tell them, "No!"

My ears started ringing and all I could think was, *They are wrong .. something is wrong. Something doesn't add up. This lab report can't be mine.*

I'm sure if you've tangled with that nasty cancer devil, it was the same for you. Disbelief. *Somebody is wrong. They must have the wrong samples. This can't be happening to me!*

"Are you sure this is my lab report?" I asked, shaking my head with incredulity. I gathered my things to leave, needing to escape that room as quickly as I could.

Sometimes your
heart needs more
time to accept
what your mind
already knows.

—Unknown

Chapter Four

Destiny Comes Before Diagnosis

My response, coming from the very heart of me was, *I'm not going into the operating room next week and that's that!* On the fourteenth of September I was scheduled to board a plane headed to Cardiff, Wales. On the nineteenth of September I was to step into the pulpit to minister. "I will deal with this when I get back," I said out loud, to no one in particular. I needed to declare my decision. I needed time to get the mind of the Lord and to tell my family. I needed time to absorb all this information. A mastectomy was a radical move. It wasn't a decision I could swallow without weighing all the options and praying through.

Even in the dictionary, destiny comes before diagnosis, I thought. "To Wales it is," I decided. I would delay any treatment until I had completed my mission.

Telling my family before I left for Wales was interesting, to say the least. When I told my husband about the diagnosis, his response to me was, "Look at it this way, dear. You'll be in a better place."

His words stunned me. I looked him in the eyes and these words rose up out of me: "I will live out every day that was given to me by God before I was born, not one second less."

My faith statement seemed to fall on deaf ears. I was not believed. "Nice bravado," he said, "but this is serious."

But I was serious! More so than any of them could ever imagine. I stated my seriousness. You see, I got mad. Not at people or at circumstances, but at the enemy of my soul, who was also the enemy of my destiny. The devil sends things to stop your destiny. FEAR is one of his greatest tools. He uses it and other tools together powerfully trying to stop us.

The important thing was, I had decisions to make and a family to consider. I needed to make sure all were well-informed. I had to make extremely important decisions in a brief period of time. And in my situation, I had to pretty much make them alone.

I needed to be careful, I knew it was easy to fall victim to the pressure that the devil brings to bear in this kind of life situation. At times, I felt like I had many plates in the air, trying to keep them all spinning at once, nervous they would come crashing down and break into smithereens!

I took my stand in faith, believing that God was with me through every step of this battle that was coming. Then I left for Cardiff and had a life-changing experience walking through the door of my destiny.

I took my stand in faith, believing that God was with me through every step of this battle that was coming.

I felt the presence—the anointing of God—strongly when I began to minister there. I felt the angel of grace move in and stand at my right side. The angel stood just behind my right shoulder and leaned in toward me. I knew I had been given an extra measure of grace. I drew great comfort and strength from that presence and I taught about extra measures of grace! When I asked who wanted prayer, everyone came forward!

I never shared with the pastors there what was going on. The medical condition was newly diagnosed, and I didn't want anything to distract from my purpose in being there. I didn't want cancer to have any attention.

You see, I knew what God had for me, and the devil had laid cancer in my path. I was determined not to have what I knew was my destiny destroyed by that thief, especially when I was just walking through that door of destiny.

Not everyone can or should make the decision I did to delay further medical actions. It is imperative that each person look in their heart to that place where they know they can hear God, rising far above their own human ability or strength. The decision was very personal and completely mine to make, just as yours is or was for you.

Chapter Five

Fear in the Night

During that two week trip to Wales, I experienced fear coming at me in the night like I had never felt before. Fear is a huge part of any battle with disease, but with cancer it is a surging, imposing force that comes at you ferociously. That spirit of fear actually stood over my bed and roared, baring its teeth at me. It was a thick tangible thing I felt come into the room. As I woke up, I commanded it to go in Jesus' name. Jesus has given us authority to use His name to make these things leave.

It tried several times to come back to torment me again, but each time it was weaker. The last time it tried, I shouted,

"I told you to go in Jesus' name!" It finally left and did not return.

Believe me, terrible things come into your mind. Tormenting feelings of grief and choking fear. Also for me, I was embarrassed and ashamed because I had cancer in my body. It was a sneaky devil, this fear. Cloaked in a shroud of shame it came with accusations. After all, you're a minister and you have cancer. Shame and guilt tried to swallow me. How would people ever trust me to pray for them? What if people knew ... blah blah blah. The enemy, how he lies and blows things up to look big, very real, and horrible. He is good at it; he's had a lot of practice.

You see, part of what tormented me was the idea that here I was a minister of the gospel, fully believing in divine healing and still do, yet I had cancer. I have worked in the medical arena, and I know that God does also use doctors, surgical procedures, and medicines to heal. He gave man the knowledge to develop these things. Jesus himself chose Luke, a physician, to be one of His disciples.

But, even knowing all of this, I still struggled with the idea of surgical intervention. This is what kept playing over and over in my thoughts: *I am a minister. I have laid hands on the sick and they have recovered. I move in the gifts of healing by the Holy Spirit, and here I have cancer in my own body.*

What the enemy was telling me was that I should be able to just stand on the Word of God and be healed without even considering medical help. That, my friend, was simply a crafty lie designed to keep me focused on the cancer and the battle.

This is a great time for a brief history lesson. I learned of this by reading a book, *God's Generals: Why They Succeeded and Why Some Failed* by Dr. Roberts Liardon (Whitaker House, New Kensington, PA, ©1996, pp. 21-44). In the 1800s there lived a Reformer Revivalist named John Alexander Dowie, dubbed "The Healing Apostle." Dowie sat under the most brilliant surgeons of his day. He learned that by the surgeons' own confessions they could not heal, only remove diseased organs, etc.

The medical practice at that time was very primitive. The doctors did not even wash their hands between patients or surgeries. Many people actually died from the lack of simple hygiene practices among doctors and surgeons. Dowie watched many surgeries not end well, witnessing the great pain from these or the death of the patients.

He began to speak of this from the pulpit, telling people not to go to doctors for help because of the dangers it presented to them. He taught that believers should go to the Word of

God only and not to doctors or medicine when they were sick. Because of the condition of the medical practice at that time, various denominations joined in this belief. It therefore became taboo to trust doctors or medicine when it came to a need for healing. It was seen as not trusting God.

Today, there are still many who will teach this as truth without ever realizing that this is where that originated. Dowie has gone down in history for his outspoken stand against the medical field.

Back to my story. So you can see how this erroneous belief made its way down to me nearly two hundred years later without my even knowing where it came from. It was freeing for me to finally learn the historical roots of this now "religious lie" that tries to hold people away from all that God has made available to them. Yes, there are healing miracles, but God also works with your medical professionals to bring about healing. He does not get mad at you for going to your doctors!

The interesting thing was that, during the two weeks I was in Wales ministering, people would come up to me for prayer and whisper in my ear that they had cancer. Then they would tell me where it was in their bodies. They had no idea what I was dealing with in my own life. I felt their pain as strongly as I felt my own trauma, and I would whisper in their ear, "I understand."

Anger would rise up in me at what the enemy was trying to do to these sweet people. I would curse that thing in the name of Jesus and command it to wither and die. Then I would share with them my understanding of the things that would come at them—fears in the night, discouragement, anger, overwhelm, a sense of loss of who they were, abandonment, to name a few. And I shared with them how to fight all of it.

I tell you these things because cancer touches your identity. It comes to steal, kill, and destroy. You are no longer who you were before the diagnosis. It changes you. You are at the point of becoming a victim. Yes, **Cancer touches your identity.** without a fight you are a victim of that lying devil. You need to learn how to stand and fight in the very core of your being. You are digging as deep within as you can to pull that up and fight. You have to get mad at it. You have to stand on the Word of God and have it in the core of you. You are out to get the Heart of God in your situation.

There were many testimonies of people getting a marvelous report after the prayer. God gives me words of knowledge for people. If God gave me a word about their illness I would give it to them. God is faithful. You need to learn how to stand up on the inside and fight the good fight of faith—and walk in places where angels fear to tread if God tells you to! You don't ever let go. Cancer is a demonic spirit that roams the earth attaching and attacking. You have to break off that spirit and command it to leave in the name of Jesus. But … the damage it has left behind has to be dealt with.

Some people feel guilty about their anxieties and regard them as a defeat of their faith, but they are afflictions not sins.

—C.S. Lewis

Chapter Six

Time to Decide

I was blessed with a doctor who is a personal friend. Upon returning to the States, she handed me her surgical manuals (huge hardbound books) and told me she had marked everything that had to do with the type of cancer that had attacked me. (Yes, I said attacked.) I took the volumes home and the research was on. This was now decision-making time, and knowledge is a weapon!

I was compliant and did the oncology visits, the MRIs, everything that was recommended, the whole enchilada soup to nuts. All the while I was gathering the information these elements could give me to aid in making my decision.

The process was tedious. The devil was never far away with his anti-faith barbs and thoughts. You have to be careful to balance research like this with consistent doses of the Word of God! I focused on scriptures like Jeremiah 29:11, Isaiah 53:5, 1 Peter 2:24. I listened to good Christian music, allowing the lyrics to bring me to a place of peace and deeper trust in the Holy Spirit.

During this period of time, a friend of mine made an appointment for me in Atlanta with the top breast specialist in the country. I went to that appointment. To say it was a traumatic experience is a total over-simplification. They took 36 more breast tissue samples and put plastic sheeting on my breast. Then they told me to put on a sports bra when I went back to my hotel room.

Knowing what to expect so I could have been prepared would have been a real blessing. Remember, I was in Atlanta. I lived in Florida. I thought I had all the instructions I would need. But I had not been told to bring a sports bra, and after all of that, I wasn't capable of going out and getting one. I had flown in. No car. I was alone once again.

Overshadowing this inconvenience and embarrassment were the thoughts I was left thinking: *If undetectable bits of cancer are present, what if I get down the road two years and then something shows up? I could be in big trouble then, and I might not still have the options that I have now.*

I was in shock, actually—medical shock from the biopsies, emotional shock from the whole cancer diagnosis still.

The staff at the hotel brought bags of ice to my room and took special care of me. I was thankful for their kind and gentle attitude. I could easily have felt so all alone. I had angels there in human form taking care of me!

My friend wanted to have her husband come and get me, but I couldn't even begin to do what all would be required for that to happen. I finally called the airline and told them my plight; arrangements were finally made to delay my flight home. In the middle of all this, I had experienced a bleed during the night, the result of all the tests done. I ended up having to go to the doctor again.

I am telling you these things to help you understand the reason I made the very personal decision I did. It just seems to never fail that the unexpected dramas manage to pop up. I think sometimes their sole purpose is to throw us off and knock us off our faith stand.

I cried out to God to guide me and to bring the spotlight of the Holy Spirit to highlight what was not for me. I had received the report from those 36 tissue samples. I had cancer in nine actual places involving that breast. An option was given for chemo and radiation. In my case it would have compromised my heart and a lung due to complications from an accident I had been in years earlier. I did not have any peace about it. When I left there I thought I was going to throw up. I knew that this course of treatment was not for me.

And then the time arrived when I had to announce my final decision. With all the information gathered, I shocked all the doctors by telling them I had decided to do bilateral mastectomies. Since there was fibrocystic disease and calcification in the other breast that could turn sour within three to five years, it was, in my opinion, the wisest choice. Please understand me. The Holy Spirit didn't tell me to do this specifically, but I had great peace knowing God had me and would be with me. I knew I wanted to fulfill my destiny, not be in for more biopsies every three to six months, putting my life on hold for pathology report after pathology report. I knew what a paralyzing grip that could be. I wanted nothing more to do with it.

As I said, this is an extremely personal and frightening thing to walk through. The decision forever changes your life. Was it a medical cure? Yes. Was I prepared for the head trip it would do on me? No way.

This is an extremely personal and frightening thing to walk through

I hope you are still with me at this point. What follows is extremely important. I don't believe that my experience through all of this was that much different from what everyone else faces. It's how we deal with it as it comes that either puts us over the top or breaks us down.

Years before I was handed my diagnosis, I had four friends call me in the same week to tell me that each of them had breast cancer. I will never forget the fact that it was four of my close friends. As of this writing, I still have three of those friends living. One went home to be with the Lord after a valiant fight; she was full of dignity and grace. The experience changed me. I had seen firsthand what a devastating blow cancer can be to an individual, a marriage, a family. It somehow helped prepare me to see clearly, not knowing that I also would walk this through in my own life.

I knew I was the matriarch of my family. I had to lead by example. So I began to talk with each member of my family. My oldest daughter did not want to give it any power. We talked about clinical decisions and left it at that.

It's important for you to recognize that some of your family members may not be capable of talking about these things because they have been gripped by a fear of losing you. Every person around you goes through their own trauma at your situation. Ask them what they are feeling. Let them help you however they can. It all looks and feels so different when it touches your own family, your own body.

My granddaughters just didn't know what to think or do. One of them wouldn't come near me because she feared I was going to leave her. It took a silly little dance at a party to draw her in and show her I was still the same Me-Ma I had always been, and will be forever!

You must do what is right for you. Weigh your options, seek wise counsel, above all pray—then decide. Once you have made your decision, communicate it lovingly but firmly with those closest to you. Stand behind your decision and let your loved ones know you ask them to stand with you in your decsion.

My youngest daughter went into researching everything she could find, trying to make sure I had all the latest information. She wanted to help me in any way she could. At the time, she was working with a mid-sized pharmaceutical company that developed cancer treatments, so she had access to the research and clinical trials information. When I told her my decision, she applauded it. Her response was, "Mom, you're the most important thing, and you have made—as hard as it is—the best decision." (Just the other day, she told me that I am the bravest person she knows. Blew me away!)

Chapter Seven

My Hardest Challenges

This all brings me to the point of sharing what I call battle scars: the most difficult parts of my journey. Yes, all of the medical challenges had to be confronted, but there were many other issues that left their forever mark on my life as I faced and fought breast cancer. Let me define some of them for you.

Battle *Scar*

My family, even though they love me, was afraid of me. They were afraid of losing me. So they distanced themselves from me. As I was making difficult decisions, I no longer felt connected with them. This loneliness, added to everything else I was experiencing, was terrible. I hated it. There were feelings of isolation and abandonment. Sometimes I had to choose to walk in forgiveness with them, just to maintain my own emotional stability.

In an earlier chapter I mentioned my husband's initial words to me about going to "a better place?" Let me share a little about where he was coming from. In talking with him much later, I asked if he remembered what he had said to me that day. He said, "No." I reminded him then that his reply to my news was, "Well, dear, look at it this way; you'll be in a better place." He was dumbstruck when I said that to him.

"Well, I remember it word for word," I said, "because it was etched forever on my heart and the backs of my eyelids."

With a loving look in his eyes he answered, "I don't doubt it."

You see, his former wife went in for a biopsy and they were called into the doctor's office to get the results (never a comforting experience). She was told to get her affairs in order because she had about four to five weeks to live. She passed away in that exact timing.

When I delivered my news to him, his mind was screaming "Oh my God! I'm going to lose her!" When he heard my news, his mind went right back into that former track of thinking and experience. I now understand the battle he was going through. But at the time, for me, his response brought a great isolation to me. But it also produced a great determination: *I'll show you!* I thought, *I am determined that I will live out every day God gave me before I was born, and not a second less!*

Let me add a note here about husbands. Mine will tell you honestly, he's not a good nurse! Some men are better at this than others. Communicate what you need, but recognize that he is also traumatized and may not be able to do or be all that you expect of him. Walk in love and forgiveness toward him. God will always meet your needs, just maybe not by the means you think! Every relationship in your life is impacted by your situation. Make no mistake about that!

Battle *Scar*

When I shared my medical information with people, some did not understand where I was coming from with my bold statements about living out the number of my days. Distance again formed. Lack of trust rose up on my part for some people to have the ability to see me through what I was facing. Oh how strongly the devil tries to separate you from the flock. He is seriously going in for the kill if he can. (He always thinks he can.)

Battle *Scar*

I am no longer like everybody else, I thought, *I am inferior.* Thoughts constantly bombarded my mind, telling me lies about myself, about what other people now thought of me, about what this had done to me. The lie set in: *I am less than.*

Battle Scar: I am no longer an attractive woman. Same here, more thoughts. I would look at myself in the mirror and tears would come. No one understood what I was going through. If not for Jesus, I would have been totally alone at times in this battle. The lie is isolation. That's the battleground.

Battle *Scar*

What if…? What if I'm wrong and I'm making the wrong decision? What if I do this and I die anyway? What if something goes wrong in the process? There are things worse than death, you know. On and on it went, and when you're in the heat of the battle, there is no time for a rest, no time for a breather. I found myself turning more and more to Jesus, holding tightly to His hand, crying out to Him, "Use me to do battle for other people."

The battle for the mind when dealing with cancer is intense. It is as intense as it can be. Low self-esteem is one of the devil's weapons that takes aim at you during this experience. If you have not been faced with self-esteem issues in the middle of your fight with cancer,

The battle for the mind when dealing with cancer is intense.

then my hat's off to you. Sometimes it could be said, "My wig's off to you!" Ha! But we do move past that phase!

With reconstruction being what it is today, we have a fighting chance of looking a world better in the end than we once did. I have been through all the stages of reconstruction and have done the decoration part. What a relief it is to be finished with the process. God is faithful, even in the littlest things that matter to us!

Let me say this here and now. People will say the dumbest things without thinking sometimes. Why bother with reconstruction? Seriously? Never ever say that to anyone. It's their journey. Don't impose your views on them. Simply listen, or ask, "How did you arrive at that decision?"

For patients with insurance or Medicare, The Women's Health and Cancer Rights Act of 1998 provided for the coverage of reconstruction procedures. Medicaid coverage differs from state to state. For those who qualify under this Act, the cost for making the breasts both looking equal are covered. Check with your insurance company, Medicare, or Medicaid officials to be certain you receive this coverage if your case in qualified. Don't be cheated out of what is rightfully yours by being uninformed. Below is a link to this Act for citizens of the United States.

www.dol.gov/sites/default/files/ebsa/about-ebsa/our-activities/resource-center/publications/whcra.pdf

Battle *Scar*

I no longer felt confident as a woman, let alone an attractive woman. A diagnosis and experience like this can rip your confidence away in a single stroke. The process brings major changes to the body that play harsh games with how you see yourself and what you believe others think of you.

The thought keeps trying to burrow into your mind you're not a real woman anymore. Again, lies and lies. But you must deal with each and every one of them if you are going to come out really whole.

Battle scars piled on top of more battle scars.

Joining Forces

I do want to tell you this. My good friends were so supportive of me. One of them, upon hearing me tell her what my diagnosis was, responded by saying, "What? Repeat that; my ears have gone fuzzy. I can't understand what you're saying!" Then she said, "I'm on my way."

It is good to have someone join forces with you to stand against your enemy together! Friendship is invaluable in times like these. Other friends stepped in immediately to stand by me, watching silly movies while tears ran down our faces. We ate good food and simply laughed and cried together.

Upon my one friend's arrival, she laid hands on me (it's scriptural), and cast out a spirit of cancer. She commanded it to never come back in Jesus' name. One of my daughters was with me and she said, "Mom, I felt that thing go across my arm when it left!"

I don't want to frighten you, but there is a spirit of cancer doing work in the earth today. It's just one of the nasty demons working in the devil's dark forces. But when, with authority in the name of Jesus, it is commanded to leave, it does. However, the damage it does still remains, and that has to be dealt with in some way. No matter what, this comes right back around to the medical issue once again.

This is no lightweight thing we battle, and everyone who tangles with this spirit/disease goes through their own personal battle. There is something called generational curses, and these often manifest as diseases. This is why your doctor always asks you about your family history. Who had what. If there is disease in your line, you are at a greater risk for encountering the same problem.

A family line may contain case after case of cancer of one type or another. That needs to be broken off at the root and commanded to wither and die in the name of Jesus. Then the blood of Jesus Christ must be applied to that family blood line.

These battle scars I have listed are just some of the personal things I have encountered. There are many others. As many of you already know, there are relationship battle scars as well. We have body scars, heart scars, relationship scars, mental and emotional scars and a lot of trauma. There's so much work of the enemy against you. It's a complicated web, all designed to take you out completely. Satan's only purpose is to steal, kill, and destroy. I am so happy to report that Jesus is much bigger than any battle scar the enemy brings against any of us!

Chapter Eight

Just Between Us

I mentioned a friend who died of cancer. She had cancer in one breast and had a mastectomy. Five years later cancer was discovered in the other breast. She ultimately died from that one. I have never seen anyone go through this battle with as much dignity and grace as she did. I told her that one day, and she replied, "You know it is Jesus!" Yes, I do know that. She went home to be with Jesus, and her battle with cancer was over!

I think it is important that you realize there is NO cancer in Heaven, and that God does not put cancer on you…ever. No, not for any reason. It is from the devil … period. We pass through this life, but Heaven is our home. If someone goes Home during a battle with cancer (or any disease) it may look and feel like they lost their battle. But remember, for those who know Jesus, going Home is a blessed event. They are totally, absolutely healed and whole instantly. You always go Home victorious to the King of kings!

It's a battle for the mind as much as for anything else. I had a good friend in Wales who had cancer and she suffered. Still she came out of her bed and stood on the street corner to witness for Jesus. She managed to get souls saved! In the heat of the battle God gave her grace. We all just stared at her and marveled. She hadn't even realized she was sick, then one day she discovered she was in stage four.

The desire of her heart was to be a Nan—a grandmother. Unresponsive for several days before the birth, she hung on until the baby was born. As family members told her that she was officially a Nan to a beautiful little boy, she squeezed their hands in response. It satisfied her heart, and she went Home to Heaven later that same night.

It takes a warrior to walk through it, so welcome to the ranks! We have many things to do in our lives, and we just keep walking. I learned a lot about the warrior I am and have become. We simply decide we are going to win and keep going, even when we don't want to or feel we can't. And there is truly nothing simple about the warfare we wade through. What kind of warrior are you?

You are what matters most. Remember that. Build a strong support team of friends. Make sure that you surround yourself with positive people. People who believe like you do—that Jesus is our Healer, **You are what** the Restorer of our soul. People who **matters most.** encourage you when the battle gets hard, who lift up your hands and arms when you get weary. People who know who you are in Christ.

There is life during cancer—during discovery, during and after surgery and in recovery. There is life after cancer. Keep your eyes on life during these times. Also take a closer look at relationships that may have been broken. Offer forgiveness or ask forgiveness if it is needed. The relief that comes from your letting go of offense and granting forgiveness at the same time you are forgiving is huge. It brings more peace into your life. Especially at this time, you need to seek after peace.

I spoke earlier of destiny. I am only passing through here on this earth. Heaven is my destiny and my Home. If I can change one heart; encourage one person; bring life, hope, and freedom, then I have done my job. There are a lot of fields ripe for harvest on my road toward Home. A lot of battle scars that need to be exposed and healed in people. I am here to help, to pray, and to share with you, to walk along beside you in faith and love.

If you don't know Jesus as your living loving Savior, let's take a minute and meet Him now. Please pray this along with me:

> Jesus, I ask You to come into my heart and live with me. I thank You for Your precious blood that was shed for me and for cleansing me of my sins. Thank You for putting my name in the Lamb's Book of Life and for making Heaven my eternal home. Amen.

Battle scars. Well, we have them, but I know the Scar Healer. His name is Jesus. Let Him into those areas. Let Him shine His light for you. Maybe you've already been through the surgery and the process, but you're left feeling all the scars and trauma brought on by the whole situation. Maybe you are just beginning your battle. Either way, it is not too late to ask Jesus to come into your battle scars and change them. How He loves to love us!

> Father, in the name of Jesus, I ask You to send the Holy Spirit to come into each and every situation that comes up in the lives of those reading this. Thank You for Your guidance and love. Thank You for the confidence that, no matter what is going on, You are

right here with us. We belong to You. Thank You for Your peace. Amen.

Let me close by saying peace and love to you. With all confidence I tell you that there is no battle you will ever face in which God cannot reach into your heart and give you peace. He will walk every step of the way beside you. You can confidently say, "Lucifer, bite the dust!"

At any given moment
you have the power
to say this is not
how the story is
going to end.

—Unknown

Chapter Nine

How You Can Help A Loved One Fighting Cancer

Many times for many reasons, cancer brings a sense of isolation and abandonment. These feelings are real and are designed by the devil as part of his plan to steal, kill, and destroy. Family members and/or friends who are willing to stand close and participate in the battle with you are a priceless blessing from the Lord!

I had friends who had cancer long before my journey began. I would get prayer cloths for them, suggest they go to a church that had healing rooms where people would anoint them with oil and pray for them, where they could listen to peaceful praise music. It connected them to others and gave them the awareness that someone had joined their journey with them and could help them talk through it as well.

What follows is a list of what I experienced in my journey. If you are the caring, compassionate, loved one wondering *what can I do to help?* use this list and let it help you come up with more things that would help your loved one.

- Hold the tissue box while she cries and talks. She needs to have a safe and loving place to express what she's experiencing.

- Be willing to take a call, a text or Facebook message at 2:00, 3:00, or 4:00 in the morning. That can be the eeriest time of night.

- Watch old movies at the same time while talking together on the phone. One of the greatest things that anyone gave me during this ordeal was the gift of their time.

- Organize meals to be delivered.

- Have prayer times with her.

- Make a list of people to call for her.

- Offer to look up medical information if she wants. Some people want to know the facts and have the information, but are not able to pull it all together. It can be a scary process. Helping with this is a very loving act.

- Look up various services that are provided in her community.

- Arrange to do fun things, silly things, anything she likes. It's a nice time to browse through photos, too.

- Give her room to have changed. Don't expect her to be exactly the same. Cancer catapults you into the next dimension. You don't really know where you will land or fit. Isolation comes. Familiar things feel surreal now. You are unsure of people's reactions to you. Patience is huge!

- Accept her where she is and accept her future.

- Be strong for her. She is both fearful and apprehensive, at the same time hopeful, needing that strong hand and heart that says, "It's going to be alright. I'm here. We can do this together."

- Offer to go grocery shopping for her or do laundry.

- Buy gifts (Christmas, birthdays, anniversaries, Hanukah, any occasion) for her to give if she feels too ill to go out. Go shopping and bring the purchases back to her. She can choose what she likes and you can return the rest. (I did this for a friend and she felt like she had shopped herself because she got to choose.) Remember, having the ability to choose in these situations empowers her. She still gets to be herself, just a little bit different than she was before.

- Offer to take her to see her aging parents or other family or friends if she can't go by herself.

- Offer to organize her kids, pack school lunches, etc.

- Bring her flowers, even chocolate if she can have it.

- Ask her if you may go to her doctor appointments with her. You can be her second set of ears. You can also help her remember to ask specific questions and jot down notes of important information. And most importantly, you can be that emotional support she needs at a very scary time.

Chapter Ten

Focus Scriptures

All from the New Living Translation

Yet it was our weaknesses he carried; it was our sorrows that weighed him down. And we thought his troubles were a punishment from God, a punishment for his own sins! But he was pierced for our rebellion, crushed for our sins. He was beaten so we could be whole. He was whipped so we could be healed.

ISAIAH 53:4-5

"For I know the plans I have for you," says the LORD. "They are plans for good and not for disaster, to give you a future and a hope.

JEREMIAH 29:11

Dear friend, I hope all is well with you and that you are as healthy in body as you are strong in spirit.

THIRD JOHN 2:2

He personally carried our sins in his body on the cross so that we can be dead to sin and live for what is right. By his wounds you are healed.

1 PETER 2:24

So you have not received a spirit that makes you fearful slaves. Instead, you received God's Spirit when he adopted you as his own children.[a] Now we call him, "Abba, Father."

ROMANS 8:15

This is why I remind you to fan into flames the spiritual gift God gave you when I laid my hands on you. For God has not given us a spirit of fear and timidity, but of power, love, and self-discipline.

2 TIMOTHY 1:6-7

Don't be intimidated in any way by your enemies. This will be a sign to them that they are going to be destroyed, but that you are going to be saved, even by God himself.

PHILIPPIANS 1:28

I tell you the truth, you can say to this mountain, 'May you be lifted up and thrown into the sea,' and it will happen. But you must really believe it will happen and have no doubt in your heart. I tell you, you can pray for anything, and if you believe that you've received it, it will be yours.

MARK 11:23-24

That evening many demon-possessed people were brought to Jesus. He cast out the evil spirits with a simple command, and he healed all the sick. This fulfilled the word of the Lord through the prophet Isaiah, who said, "He took our sicknesses and removed our diseases."

MATTHEW 8:16-17

Faith shows the reality of what we hope for; it is the evidence of things we cannot see.

MATTHEW 8:16-17

About the Author

DeAnn Clark is an ordained minister, psalmist, author, teacher, and counselor. Moving in the gifts of the Holy Spirit, she is known for the ability to zero in on what the Spirit is saying for a time such as this. It is her desire to see each person have old chains broken that have held them back and be released into their true destiny in God.

Active in the ministry for more than 30 years, she has ministered in a variety of capacities including choir director, music minister, drama and music director, worship leader, and pastor. Through the years she has been involved with Christian Retreat, Norvel Hayes Ministries, Charles and Frances Hunter, Hunter Ministries, Impact Ministries, and Kathie Walters Ministries before launching out into her own international ministry.

Growing up in a small Florida town, the only daughter of a Baptist deacon and a Sunday school teacher, DeAnn began to realize at an early age the call of God upon her life. Recognizing that this call far exceeded the boundaries of her Baptist church, she put herself into a quest for more of God. After receiving the baptism in the Holy Spirit, she began to move more fully into what she knew was written on her heart—into her destiny in the things of God.

Through the years DeAnn has touched the hearts of people from Florida to Siberia and more, continuing to walk through each door that God opens for her. Today God continues to open ministry doors for her from one corner of the world to another. She ministers in churches and other gatherings in the United States, Wales, England, France, and elsewhere. The scope of her travels continues to grow as she follows the Lord's leading.

With compassion and the Word of God, it is DeAnn's mission to bring salvation, freedom, healing, and wholeness to all who seek a deeper walk with Him.

DeAnn Clark Ministries

PO Box 1623
Palmetto, FL 34220

deannclarkministries.com
deannclarkministries@gmail.com

Titles by DeAnn Clark

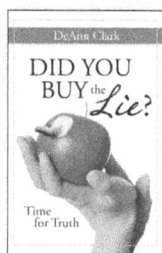

Did You Buy the Lie?

Think you know truth from lies when it comes to the things of God? Read this book to learn some of the things we blame on God that are simply not true. Freedom awaits you as you learn to recognize the lies of the enemy.

Battle Scars

This small book carries a powerful testimony of the author's personal walk through the battlefield of breast cancer. Learn how God's love and faith in Jesus, our Healer, sustained her and delivered her from all the battle scars she encountered.

Lucifer, Bite the Dust!

New Book Coming Soon!

Are you afraid of the devil? Does he have power over you? Is there anything you can do to get him out of your way? Bible-based practical answers to questions you should be asking!

Vocal Recordings by De Ann Clark

I See an Open Door

I see an Open door was recorded in the land of song, Wales, U.K. I was preparing to preach when that first line was sung as worship began. God told me that was the title of my CD. I had this argument with God because HE interrupted my review of my notes. His answer to my little speech to Him was, "Get busy.' As you can see God Won, Jeremiah 1:5 is the theme that draws you into the presence and intention of this CD.

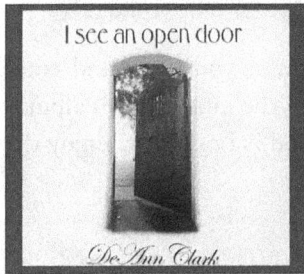

Amazed

As I was listening to music I began to paint on an easel. As the Song *I Stand Amazed In His Presence* began to play, I was struck by how truly AMAZED I was at what the Presence of God had created in the year that had passed since recording *I see An Open Door*. Amazed was conceived that night as I sang with abandon and painted. This up-beat, spirit-lifting CD will have you praising and rejoicing.

Pour the Oil

The Lord spoke to me some time ago about recording a healing album. I said, "Yes," … and waited for His timing. The title song in this collection was birthed in my heart as I was ministering one night. Heaven moved on me and the song, Pour the Oil, came forth. I knew God was saying, "It's time!" In the same way that I encountered Heaven that night, God also wants you to encounter Him as you listen and enter into His presence. His anointing and love is in the music of this album. It is His will to heal, to refresh, to restore. God is Love only. Enjoy the peace and the journey!

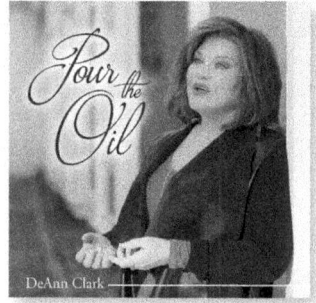

www.ingramcontent.com/pod-product-compliance
Lightning Source LLC
Chambersburg PA
CBHW060422050426
42449CB00009B/2092